Contraptions

By Harriet Hodgson
Illustrated by Susan Cronin-Paris

Publisher: Roberta Suid
Editor: Bonnie Bernstein
Design: Susan Pinkerton
Production: Mary McClellan
Cover Design: David Hale
Cover Art: Philip Chalk

 MM975

Monday Morning is a registered trademark
of Monday Morning Books, Inc.

Entire contents copyright © 1987 by Monday Morning
Books, Inc., Box 1680, Palo Alto, California 94302

ISBN 0–912107–59–6

Printed in the United States of America

9 8 7 6 5 4 3 2 1

Contents

Introduction

Contraption. What a great-sounding word! My dictionary says a contraption is a gadget, something makeshift, often silly. This book tells how kids can make use of whatever's around to slap together a bunch of kooky things that really work: contraptions!

MATERIALS

Contraptions are made from ordinary, throw-away stuff, like plastic milk cartons and coffee cans. Many materials can be used over and over again, so that when you've gathered the materials for one project, you may have what you need for another. Your kids will also need some basic tools and supplies—scissors, hole punch, brass fasteners, white glue, etc.—and some household items, such as trash bag ties and Styrofoam cups.

Read the materials list and directions before starting a project. If you don't have all the exact materials, find safe substitutes. Canning jar lids do just as well as the lids that come on peel-strip juice cans, and kids can bend their own wire handle if you don't happen to have one from an ice cream bucket. Substitutes will make the contraptions all the more interesting and inventive.

SAFETY AND SUPERVISION

Check the safety of materials you or the children collect. Don't use metal cans with sharp edges, plastic bottles that once held chemicals, or anything made of glass. Permanent markers should always be used in a well-ventilated room.

An adult should help children make contraptions that require using a hammer, hand saw, hand drill, kitchen shears, and grapefruit knife. Some children may be able to handle these tools themselves, but you won't be regarded as interfering if you stand by to help hold a wobbly part or applaud when the contraption works.

Don't supervise too closely. If your children want to make something a little differently, or turn one contraption into another, encourage their originality. It's the fun that counts!

Adjustable Hurdle

WHAT YOU NEED:
2 coffee cans with plastic lids
Kitchen shears
2 yardsticks (sometimes free from hardware stores)
Soil, gravel, or sand
Clothespins (any kind)
Twig

WHAT YOU DO:
1. Cut a small slit in the center of each coffee can lid. The slits should be as wide as the ends of the yardsticks.
2. Hold a yardstick upright in center of each can. Pour in soil, gravel, or sand to weigh down cans.
3. Slide plastic lids down over the yardsticks, then snap lids onto rims of cans.
4. Space clothespins (pegs) every two inches along yardsticks.
5. Set cans on grass. Rest twig across lowest pegs. Jump the hurdle, raising the twig a peg each time.

Balancing Act

WHAT YOU NEED:
Handsaw
Dowel
Sandpaper or sanding sponge
2 scraps of wood the same width
White glue
Wire
Wire ice cream bucket handle
Washers (rubber or metal)
2 paper clips

WHAT YOU DO:
1. Saw the dowel in half. Sand the rough edges.
2. Glue each dowel onto a wood scrap. Let the glue dry.
3. Wind ends of wire around dowels.
4. Bend ice cream bucket handle until rounded. Balance handle on wire.
5. Hang a washer on each end of the handle.
6. Unbend paper clips in the middle to form an *S* shape. Use clips to link more washers onto each side. How long can you keep up your Balancing Act?

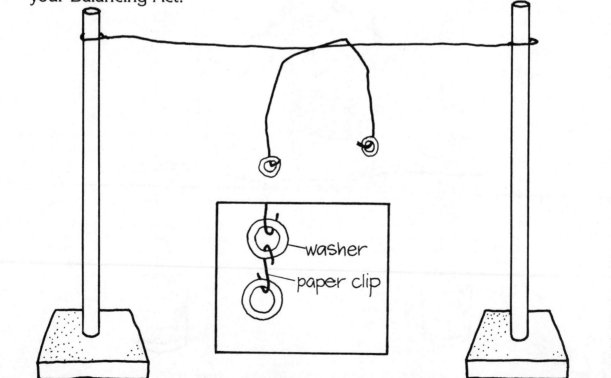

washer

paper clip

Battery-Powered Magnet

WHAT YOU NEED:
20 feet of thermostat wire (two- or three-strand)
3-inch bolt
2 washers that fit bolt
Nut that fits bolt
6-volt battery
Small steel or iron objects (such as paper clips, nails, and needles)

WHAT YOU DO:
1. Separate one strand from the thermostat wire.
2. Put one washer on bolt head, one on bolt end, then screw on bolt.
3. Leaving a foot-long tail, wind four layers of wire around the bolt as tightly as you can.
4. Peel away a bit of plastic coating on both ends of the wire.
5. Loosen black buttons on top of battery. Place a wire under each button and tighten buttons.
6. Pick up objects with your electromagnet. This magnet is so strong it will even pick up a pair of pliers! Be sure to unfasten wires when you're done. (Do not use your electromagnet near a watch that has gears.)

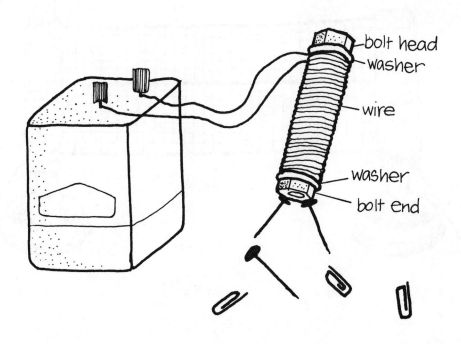

bolt head
washer
wire
washer
bolt end

Best Net Yet

WHAT YOU NEED:
2 small plumbing plungers with 4-inch diameters
Polyester/cotton mesh (6-inch strip of 60-inch wide fabric)
Strapping tape
Small rubber ball

WHAT YOU DO:
1. Tape ends of netting to plunger handles.
2. Wind netting around handles like a scroll until net is the width of your playing table.
3. Position net across plastic or metal table. Push down on plungers to create suction so net will stay in position.
4. Players hit ball with palm of hand across net. When one player misses, the other scores a point.

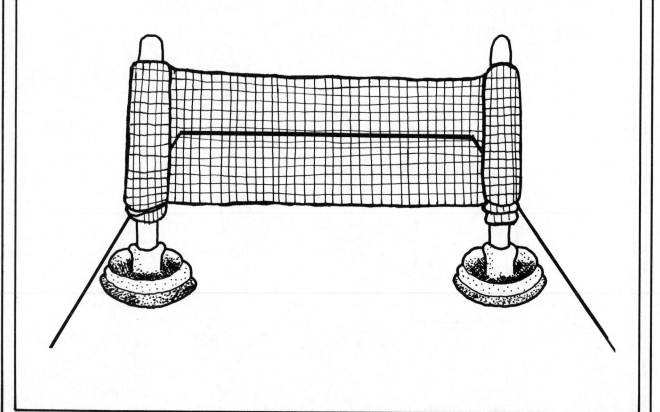

Bird Feeder

WHAT YOU NEED:
2 plastic berry baskets
Kitchen shears
¾ cup mixed bird seed
Peanut butter (about 3 tablespoons)
Small bowl
Spoon
Table knife
Waxed paper
4 twist ties
1 plastic trash bag tie
Stick

WHAT YOU DO:
1. Cut one row of squares off each berry basket.
2. Mix bird seed and peanut butter together in small bowl. Add just enough peanut butter to hold seed together.
3. Lay one berry basket on waxed paper. Pat seed mixture into bottom with table knife.
4. Fit rim of second basket inside first.
5. Fasten baskets together at corners with twist ties.
6. Slip plastic tie through top-center of feeder. Hang feeder on a tree.
7. Push stick through seed mixture for a perch.

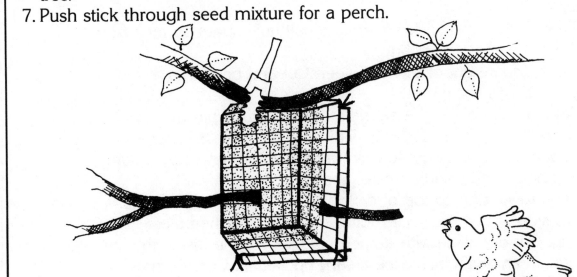

Boat-Car-Plane Transformer

WHAT YOU NEED:
Large cardboard box with flaps
Grapefruit knife
Oatmeal carton
Construction paper (12" x 18")
White glue
Scissors
Nail
Paper towel tube
Cardboard potato chip can
File folder
3 brass fasteners
Strapping tape
Ballpoint pen
Plastic lid from ice cream bucket
Narrow board or cardboard (longer than width of box)

WHAT YOU DO:
1. Fold three flaps to inside of box for added support. Fold out fourth flap.
2. Trim outside flap with a grapefruit knife to make it triangular. This is the front of your transformer.
3. Glue construction paper around the oatmeal carton to hide label.
4. Turn carton upside down. Poke a nail hole about an inch from the open end of the carton.
5. Cut a square out of the file folder. Cut and bend into a pinwheel as shown.
6. Poke a nail hole in the oatmeal carton. Attach pinwheel to carton with a brass fastener. This is your outboard motor.
7. Attach oatmeal carton to box (pinwheel end down) by poking nail holes and inserting brass fasteners.
8. Tape towel tube to top of carton to make motor handle.
9. On side of box opposite motor, trace around the potato chip can. Cut out circle with grapefruit knife, staying inside the line.
10. Trace can again inside ice cream bucket lid. Cut out circle.

11. Push can through hole in box. Fit plastic lid on end of can for steering wheel.
12. Transform into three vehicles: sit in back by outboard motor for boat; sit in front by steering wheel for car; or lay board across box for wings of plane.

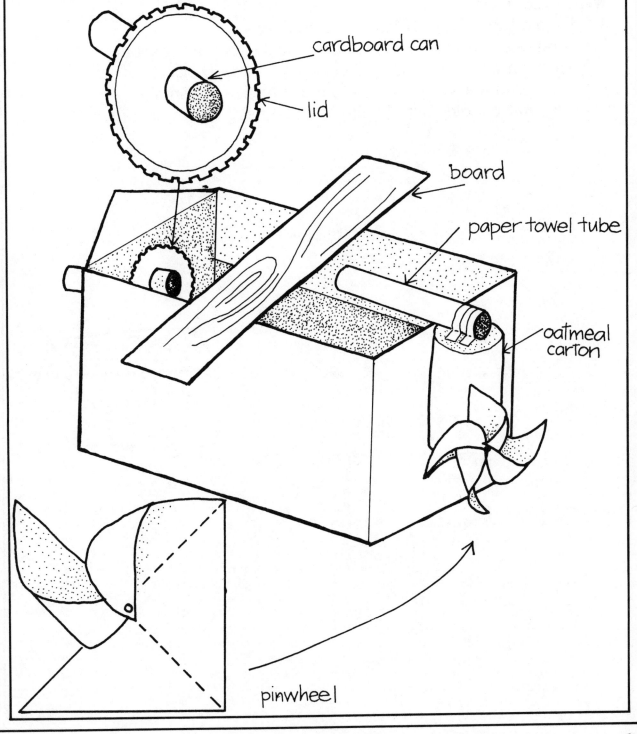

cardboard can

lid

board

paper towel tube

oatmeal carton

pinwheel

Brickmaker

WHAT YOU NEED:
Half-gallon milk carton (cardboard)
Kitchen shears
Strapping tape

WHAT YOU DO:
1. Pry open top of milk carton. Rinse and dry.
2. Cut off one side of carton, including the flap part from spout.
3. Fold down other three flaps to close end. Tape in place.
4. Use mold in wet sand or snow to make bricks. For smaller bricks, make molds out of half-pint or pint-size cream cartons.

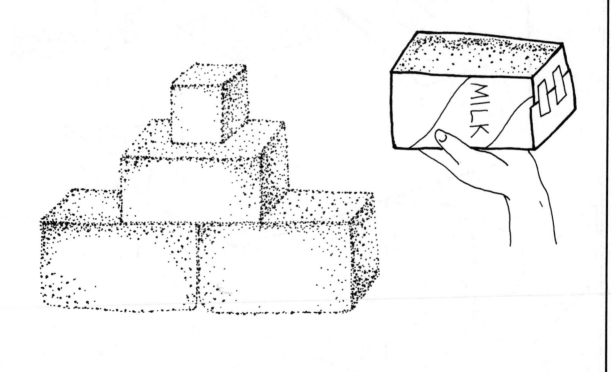

Broomstick Tetherball

WHAT YOU NEED:
3 lb. coffee can with plastic lid
Scissors
Soil, gravel, or sand
Old broomstick
1 yard heavy twine
Small piece of nylon netting or an old sock
Blunt needle
Small ball

WHAT YOU DO:
1. Cut a small circle out of center of plastic lid (roughly the same diameter as the broomstick).
2. Hold broomstick upright in center of can. Pour in soil, gravel, or sand to weigh down can.
3. Slide plastic lid down over broomstick, then snap onto rim of can.
4. Tie one end of twine to top of broomstick.
5. Thread other end of twine through needle. Gather netting tightly around ball. Weave twine through netting and knot. (Or place ball inside sock, gather tightly, and knot. Then tie twine to sock.)
6. Two players stand across from each other. Players hit ball with hands or wooden paddles in opposite directions. Who can make the twine coil completely around the pole?

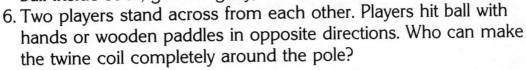

Bucket Base Fiddle

WHAT YOU NEED:
Galvanized metal bucket or old metal wastepaper basket
Old broomstick
Hand saw
Hammer
Nail
String
Washer (metal or rubber)

WHAT YOU DO:
1. Saw a slit across bottom end of broomstick.
2. Saw a slit around broomstick, about an inch from top end.
3. Turn bucket upside down. Hammer nail hole in center of bucket.
4. Cut length of string slightly longer than broomstick. Tie one end around top slit. Push other end down through hole in bucket and tie onto washer. (Washer is on inside of bucket.)
5. Perch slit end of broomstick on bottom rim of bucket.
6. Hold top of broomstick with one hand and place one foot on bucket to steady it. Pluck string with fingers on other hand to make music. Change pitch by bending handle at different angles. Accompany yourself by singing or blowing a whistle!

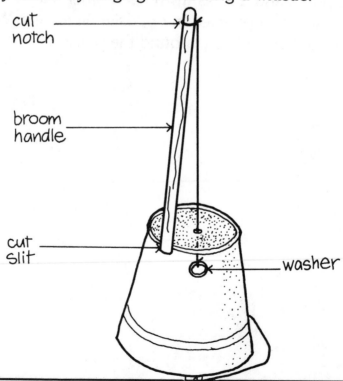

cut notch

broom handle

cut slit

washer

Cardboard Mannequin

WHAT YOU NEED:
2 panels from large corrugated cardboard box
Pencil
Grapefruit knife
Nail
4 brass fasteners (largest size)
Crayons

WHAT YOU DO:
1. Lie down on one panel. Have someone trace around your body in pencil, leaving out your arms. Have that person trace each arm on the other panel.
2. Use grapefruit knife to cut out mannequin body and arms.
3. Cut arms in half at elbows.
4. Refasten upper and lower parts of arms with brass fasteners, using nail to poke necessary holes. Also attach arms to body with brass fasteners.
5. Draw face and hair.
6. Dress mannequin in your clothes. Position arms in a natural pose, or shake hands with yourself!

Cylinder Shelves

WHAT YOU NEED:
5-gallon cardboard ice cream cartons (free from ice cream store)
Giant bobby pins or jumbo paper clips
Contact paper or color markers

WHAT YOU DO:
1. Rinse and dry ice cream cartons.
2. Cover cartons with contact paper or decorate with markers.
3. Set three cartons on their sides. Fasten rims together with the bobby pins or paper clips.
4. Stack another two cartons on top of the first three, pyramid-fashion. Fasten to first row with more pins or clips.
5. Store toys, clothes, and supplies in shelves. Heavier items should go in bottom shelves.

Dandy Discus

WHAT YOU NEED:
2 plastic ice cream bucket lids

WHAT YOU DO:
1. Wash and dry the lids.
2. Fit one lid inside the other, pressing edges.
3. Throw discus into grass or roll on the sidewalk.

Dumper

WHAT YOU NEED:
2 cardboard soda trays
Cardboard box slightly smaller in length and width than soda trays
   (with all sides intact)
Kitchen shears
White glue
Cardboard tube from wire pants hanger
Nail
String or long shoelace

WHAT YOU DO:
1. Poke two nail holes in the end of one soda tray. Thread strings through the holes and tie.
2. Fit second soda tray inside the first soda tray to form sturdy base.
3. Cut top and back panels off box with kitchen shears.
4. Glue bottom of box to base.
5. Fold down an inch-wide rim at both ends of top panel. Insert one folded rim in slit formed in front of base where soda trays fit together.
6. Squeeze line of glue along top-front edge of box. Glue other rim down on this edge.
7. Glue tube from hanger to one end of back panel removed in step 2 to make dumper.
8. Cut two small, V-shaped notches in sides near top-back corners of box. Fit dumper into notches.
9. Load up dumper with small lightweight toys. Lift and dump load.

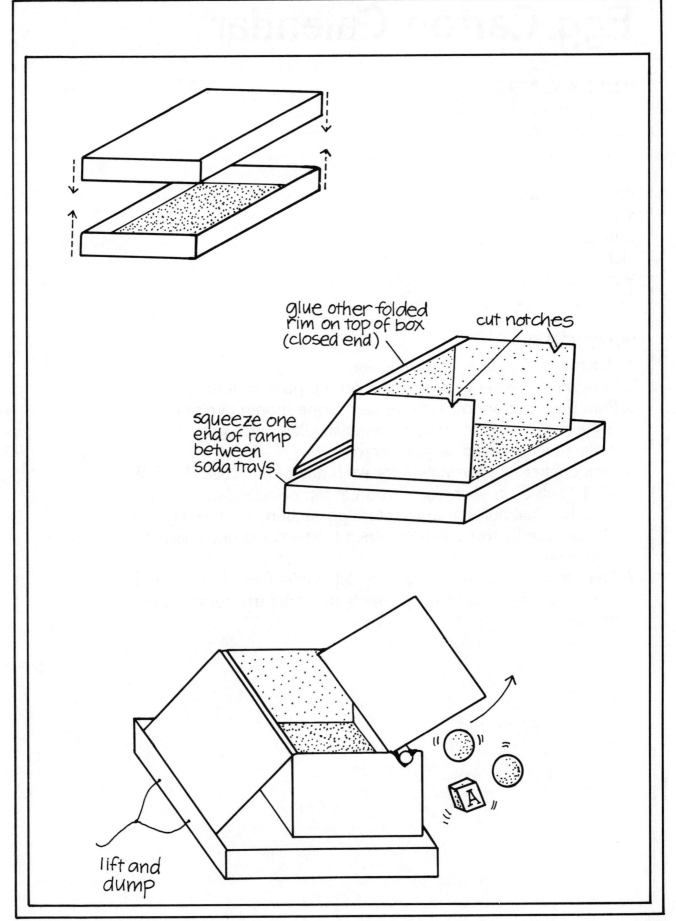

glue other folded
rim on top of box
(closed end)

cut notches

squeeze one
end of ramp
between
soda trays

lift and
dump

Egg Carton Calendar

WHAT YOU NEED:
31 caps from plastic milk cartons
Permanent marker
12 file cards
2 egg flats
Kitchen shears
White glue
Spring-type clothespin
Nail
Wire trash bag tie
Calendar

WHAT YOU DO:
1. Wash and dry caps. Peel off labels.
2. Print numerals on caps with marker, numbering from 1-31.
3. Print names of months on file cards, one month per card.
4. Cut a row of egg sections off one flat. Glue onto other flat to make rows of seven sections across.
5. Print a letter or abbreviation for each day of the week (M, T, W, Th, F, Sat, S) in each egg section at top of calendar.
6. Poke two nail holes in top center egg section (Wednesday). Thread wire tie through holes, then twist around one shaft of clothespin.
7. Snap appropriate month card in clothespin. Refer to a calendar to put numbered caps in egg sections under the correct days of the week.

Endless Chain

WHAT YOU NEED:
Notched trash bag ties
Scissors
2 wire hangers

WHAT YOU DO:
1. Gather as many trash bag ties as you can. Link them together.
2. Cut off points of ties with scissors so they don't tickle you.
3. Hook clothes hanger through link at each end of chain.
4. Chain off a special section of room, or hook ends to chairs and jump over, or make shapes on floor. Add more links as you collect more ties—a truly endless project.

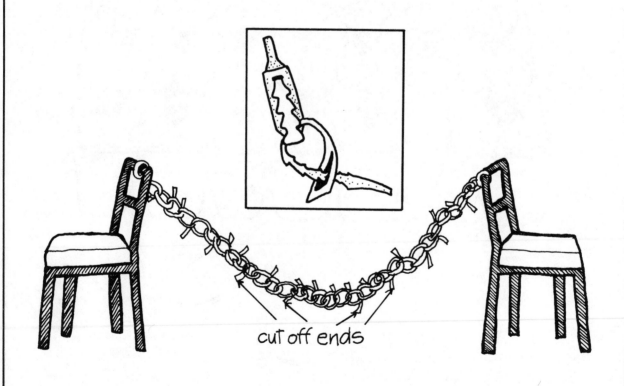

cut off ends

Flash Signal System

WHAT YOU NEED:
Flashlight
Plastic lids (different colors)
File cards
Watercolor markers

WHAT YOU DO:
1. Wash and dry lids if necessary.
2. Decide on your signals. For example: One red flash means "Come over and play." Two red flashes mean "Bring a snack," etc.
3. Draw pictures to illustrate each signal on file cards. Make two sets of cards: one for the sender; one for the receiver.
4. Hold colored lid in front of lighted flashlight to send signals.

Floating Compass

WHAT YOU NEED:
Margarine tub
Blunt needle
Magnet (bar or horseshoe)
Styrofoam cup
Scissors

WHAT YOU DO:
1. Wash and dry margarine tub.
2. Rub needle in *one direction only* across a bar magnet. If using a horseshoe magnet, rub needle from center down *one side only.* Rub several times to magnetize needle.
3. Cut bottom off Styrofoam cup, leaving ¼"-½" rim.
4. Cut two narrow notches opposite each other in cup rim. Check that needle fits comfortably in notches, then remove it.
5. Fill margarine tub halfway with water.
6. Float cup in tub. Gently lay needle across center of cup. Watch the compass quickly spin to north-south!

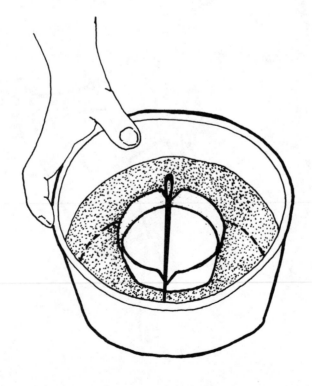

Great Gong

WHAT YOU NEED:
Pizza pan
Hammer
Nail
Old tube sock
String (about 18 inches)
Wooden spoon
Scissors
Polyester stuffing
Rubber band

WHAT YOU DO:
1. Make a hole near the rim of the pizza pan with hammer and nail.
2. Loop string through hole and knot.
3. Cut off sock from the ankle up.
4. Cover rounded part of wooden spoon with sock foot. Stuff polyester around spoon bowl until sock foot is round.
5. Secure stuffed sock around spoon handle with rubber band. This is your mallet. Hit the pizza pan with the mallet. Baauum!

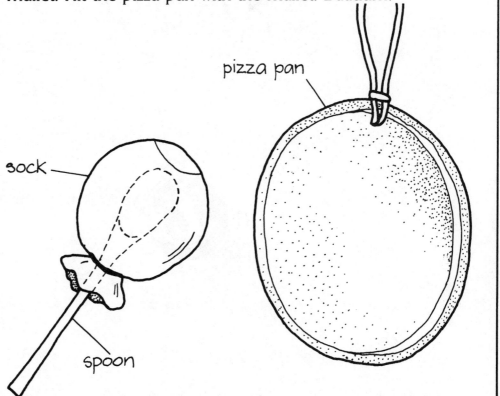

pizza pan

sock

spoon

Horizontal Yo-Yo

WHAT YOU NEED:
Cardboard tubes from two wire pants hangers
Twine (about 30")
Yo-yo

WHAT YOU DO:
1. Tie each end of twine to a cardboard tube.
2. Remove string from yo-yo.
3. Set yo-yo on twine. Hold a tube in each hand. Balancing carefully, swing yo-yo from tube to tube.

Lighted Tracing Box

WHAT YOU NEED:
Corrugated box without top
Piece of clear acrylic larger than length and width of box
Nail
String
Pencil
Flashlight
Pictures to trace
Typing paper

WHAT YOU DO:
1. Poke two nail holes in top corner of box (left corner for righties, right corner for lefties).
2. Tie one end of string through holes, and other end onto pencil.
3. Turn on flashlight and set upright in bottom of box.
4. Lay acrylic plate on top of box. Place picture on plate, and typing paper on top of picture. Trace picture. Remember to turn off flashlight when you're done.

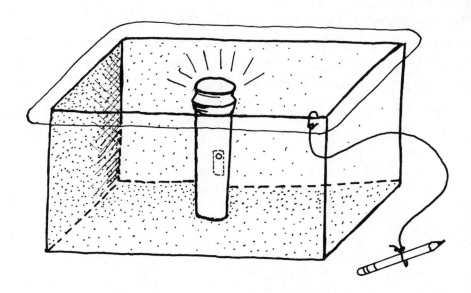

Magnetic Theater

WHAT YOU NEED:
Shoebox
Kitchen shears
Nail
2 brass fasteners
Styrofoam spools
Comics pages
White glue
Small piece of cardboard
Thumbtacks
Small magnet

WHAT YOU DO:
1. Remove lid from shoebox. Turn box upside down. Cut off one long side panel, leaving a half-inch margin along each side so box stays sturdy.
2. Cut off rim on one long side of box lid.
3. Attach lid to box with brass fasteners as shown. Poke nail holes before inserting fasteners.
4. Glue favorite comic strips onto cardboard. Let dry.
5. Cut out individual animals and people.
6. Make a slit in one end of each spool with table knife. Stand a comics character in each spool.
7. Push two thumbtacks into bottom of each spool.
8. Place characters on shoebox stage. Make characters strut and spin by moving the magnet along the underside of the stage. If you like, draw scenery cards to fit back of stage and attach with paper clips.

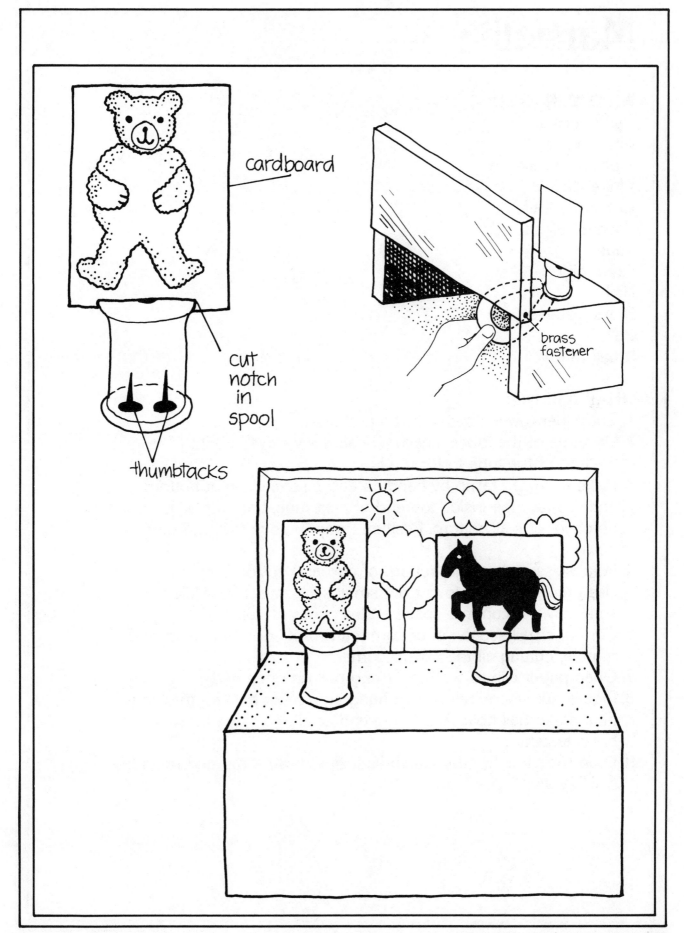

cardboard

cut notch in spool

thumbtacks

brass fastener

Marbell

WHAT YOU NEED:
Cardboard soda tray
Kitchen shears
2 paper towel tubes
White glue
Grapefruit knife
Tapered plastic cup
Tape
Paper clip
Nail
Brass fastener
Bell
Small marble

WHAT YOU DO:
1. Cut paper towel tubes in half lengthwise.
2. On three of the tubes, cut away half the width to about 2″ from the end of the tube to form a tab.
3. Make a zig-zag ramp by bending and inserting tab at bottom end of one tube inside top end of next tube, finishing with notched tube at bottom. Position ramp in soda tray and glue down.
4. Poke scissors through bottom of cup and cut off bottom.
5. Use grapefruit knife to cut out small section in upper left rim of soda tray. Fit cup into space and secure with tape.
6. Cut out small section in bottom left rim of soda tray for exiting marble, cutting all the way to corner.
7. Open paper clip to S shape. Hang bell on open end.
8. Figure out where bell should hang above exit hole so marble will hit it. Poke nail hole. Attach top end of clip to side of tray with brass fastener.
9. Drop marble into cup. Watch as it zips down ramp and rings the bell. Ta-da!

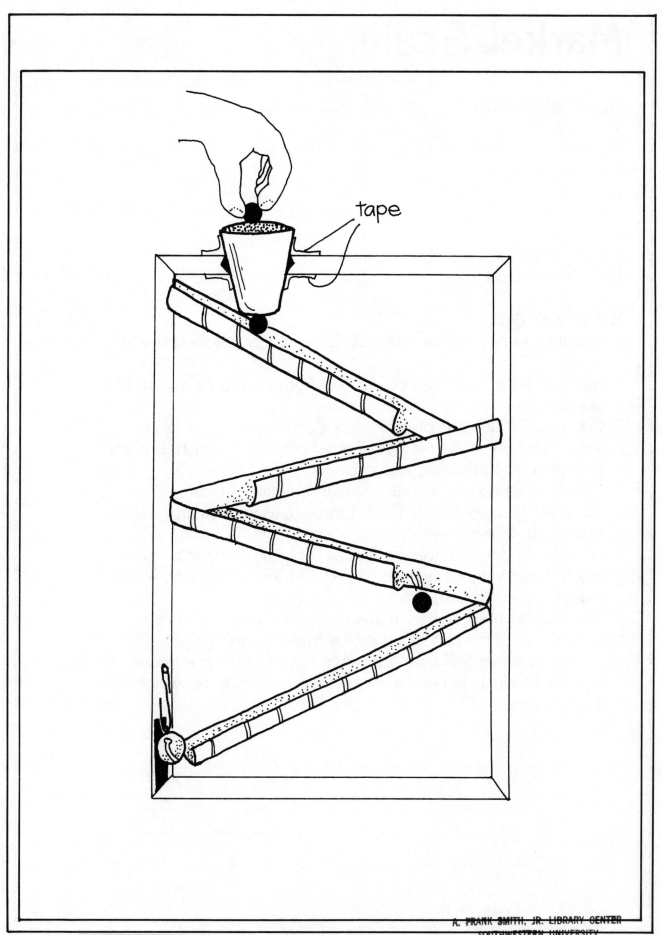

tape

Market Scale

WHAT YOU NEED:
Yardstick
Hand drill
Metal pie pan
Hammer
Nail
String
Fishing weight (largest you can find)
Permanent marker

WHAT YOU DO:
1. Drill hole in one end of yardstick. Drill a second hole at the 11″ mark.
2. Hammer three nail holes equidistant from each other in rim of pie pan.
3. Cut three 20″ lengths of string. Knot one end of each piece through a hole in the pie pan. Gather other ends, push through hole at end of yardstick, and knot.
4. Loop and tie a string handle through hole at 11″ mark.
5. Cut a 12″ piece of string. Thread through loop of fishing weight. Knot ends. Slip onto yardstick.
6. Place second fishing weight in pan. Lift scale by handle. Slide first weight along yardstick until pan and weight balance. Mark that place on the yardstick.
7. Weigh other objects. How many blocks, for example, do you have to put in the pan to balance with the fishing weight? Can you mark where half a weight would balance? (Hint: Remove half the blocks.) Can you mark increments for double weight? Triple weight?

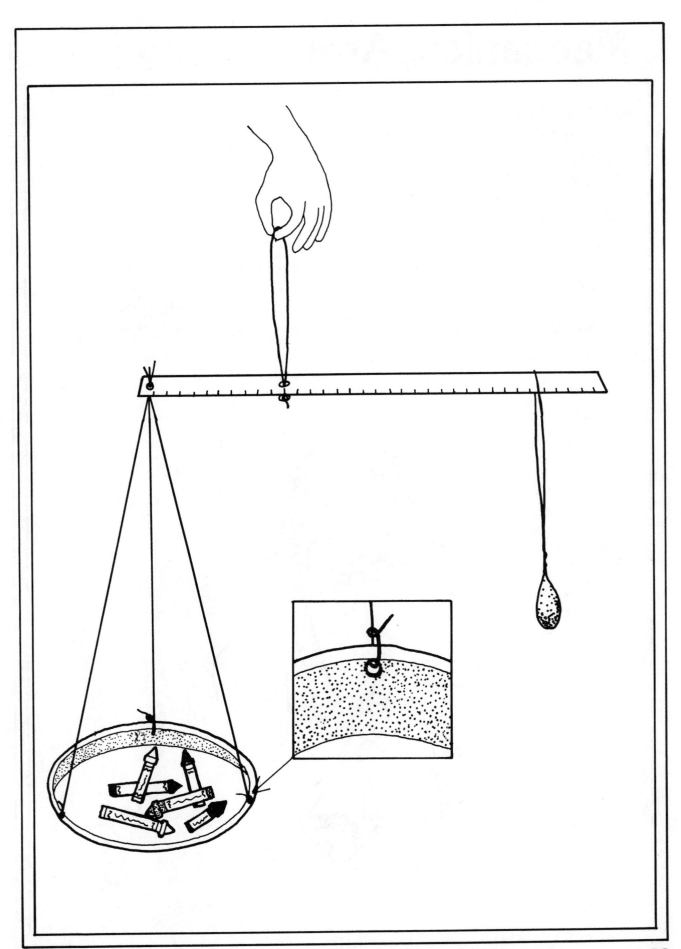

Mechanical Arm

WHAT YOU NEED:
2 yardsticks
Plastic salad tongs (scissors type)
Strapping tape

WHAT YOU DO:
1. Tape one handle of salad tongs to the end of one yardstick, winding tape around and around. Snip tape. Repeat with other handle of salad tongs and other yardstick.
2. Pick up objects with your robot arm by opening and closing the tongs. What is the smallest thing you can pick up? What is the largest?

Mighty Megaphone

WHAT YOU NEED:
Empty laundry detergent bottle with handle
Bottle opener
Kitchen shears
Small piece of poster board
Strapping tape

WHAT YOU DO:
1. Rinse and dry detergent bottle. Pry off spout with flat end of bottle opener.
2. Cut off bottom of bottle with kitchen shears.
3. Roll poster board and fit into opening at bottom of bottle. Secure with tape.
4. Speak through spout-end of bottle. Can you be heard across the room? At the other end of the block?

Milk Carton Microscope

WHAT YOU NEED:
Plastic gallon milk carton
Kitchen shears
Cardboard tube from wire pants hanger or a dowel
Nail
Large magnifying glass
Small magnifying glass (remove casing if there is one)
2 pieces of wire

WHAT YOU DO:
1. Cut neck off milk carton with kitchen shears, also cutting away a 2" collar around the neck.
2. Wash and dry milk carton. Turn upside down. Trim carton if it wobbles.
3. Poke nail hole in bottom of milk carton directly over handle. Enlarge hole by wiggling point of shears in it.
4. Insert cardboard tube or piece of dowel down into handle.
5. Twist wire around handles of magnifying glasses, leaving enough tail to twist around tube or dowel shaft.
6. Twist remaining wire around shaft. The large magnifying glass should be positioned below the small one, about an inch or two from the bottom of the milk carton.
7. Place object to be viewed under the large magnifying glass. Slide small magnifying glass along shaft until object is in focus.

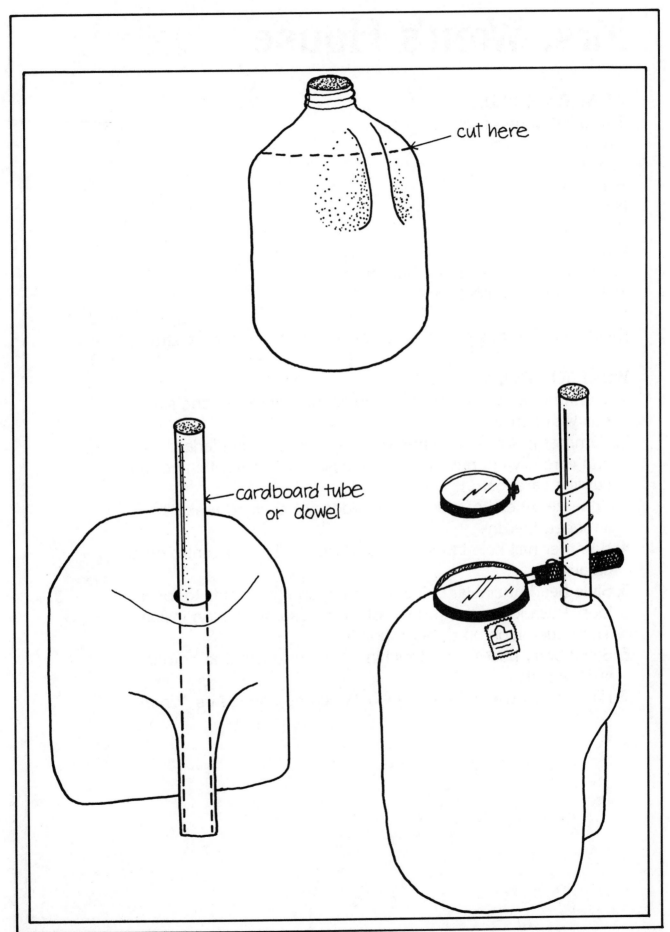

cut here

cardboard tube
or dowel

Mrs. Wren's House

WHAT YOU NEED:
2 wooden berry boxes
Quarter
Pencil
Hammer
Nail
Scissors
White glue
Lid from plastic ice cream bucket
Twist ties from trash bags
String
Bead, button with loop, or other small object that can be strung

WHAT YOU DO:
1. Turn one berry box upside down. Draw a circle on one side of box with pencil.
2. Hammer nail hole in center of circle. Fit scissors blade in hole and carefully cut out circle. (Wood sides are wafer-thin so they cut like cardboard.)
3. Squeeze a bead of glue around edges of circle to make it stronger. Let dry.
4. Hammer nail hole in top of box. Poke nail hole in center of ice cream lid.
5. Slide bead or similar object on string and knot ends to form loop. Push loop up through hole in box so bead is on inside. Then push loop up through hole in lid.
6. Stack berry boxes, rims touching. Fasten together at corners with twist ties.
7. Hang birdhouse on tree branch. Welcome home, Mrs. Wren!

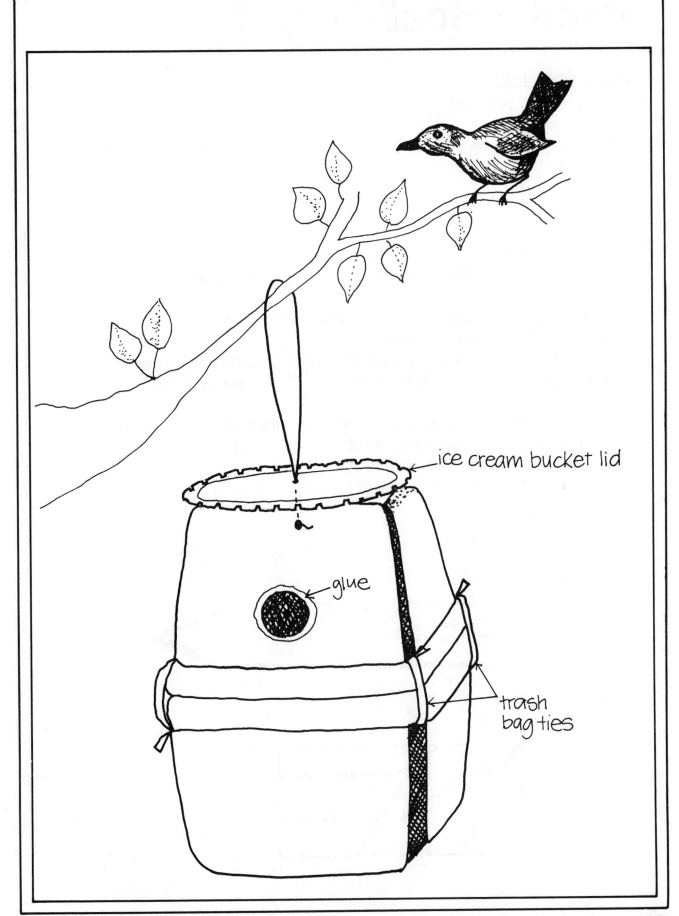

ice cream bucket lid

glue

trash bag ties

Paddle Boat

WHAT YOU NEED:
Small piece of plywood
Coping saw
Sandpaper or sanding sponge
Plastic lid
Kitchen shears
Fat rubber band

WHAT YOU DO:
1. Saw sides at one end of plywood to a point. This is the front of your boat.
2. Saw a long notch out of the other end of the boat.
3. Sand all rough edges smooth.
4. Cut long rectangle out of plastic lid. Piece should be narrower and shorter than notch in back of boat. This is your paddle wheel.
5. Stretch rubber band across back of boat. Insert paddle wheel in notched area, between sides of rubber band, and twist around and around until rubber band is taut.
6. Holding paddle wheel, place boat in water. Let go! Watch your paddle boat paddle plenty!

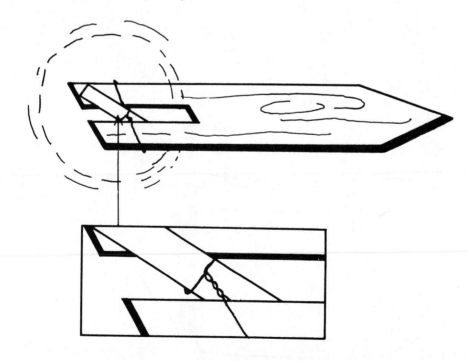

Paper Doll Parachutist

WHAT YOU NEED:
Figure on cereal box, or thin cardboard and markers
Plastic bag
Scissors
Sturdy thread, such as button twist
Cellophane tape

WHAT YOU DO:
1. Cut out large cereal box figure (toucan, tiger, cartoon character, etc.), or draw and cut your own cardboard figure.
2. Slit seams of plastic bag. Save one square.
3. Cut four pieces of thread the same length. Knot one end of each thread.
4. Tape knotted ends to corners of plastic square. Draw up other ends and knot together.
5. Tape knot to back of cardboard figure.
6. Toss figure up in the air. Watch your brave parachutist float gently down to the ground!

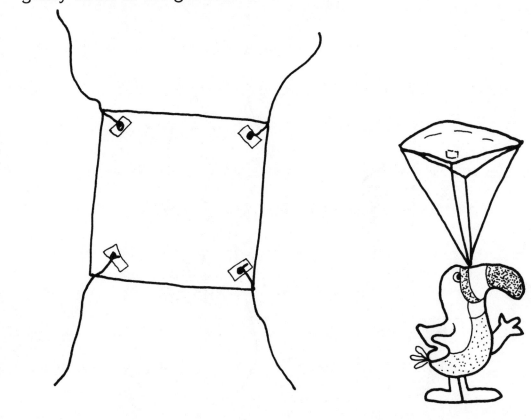

Pendulum Person

WHAT YOU NEED:
Plastic bottle (detergent, shampoo, syrup, etc.)
Cardboard tube from wire pants hanger
Grapefruit knife
Soil, gravel, or sand
Tapered plastic cup
Permanent marker

WHAT YOU DO:
1. Rinse and dry bottle.
2. Turn cup upside down. Draw on face with marker.
3. Stand cardboard tube in bottle. Fill bottle with soil, gravel, or sand.
4. Try cup head on for size. If tube is too long, cut piece off end with grapefruit knife.
5. Pinch tube top closed. Replace cup on top of tube and tap gently. Your pendulum person will nod and nod. If you like, make a whole family of pendulum people using different-sized bottles.

Pipes and Fittings

WHAT YOU NEED:

½-inch diameter assorted plastic pipes (straight, T's, elbows, couplings, 45's)
Plastic ice cream bucket with lid

WHAT YOU DO:

1. Wash and dry ice cream bucket.
2. Ask hardware store clerk to cut pipe into 1-foot, 6-inch, and 4-inch lengths.
3. Make all sorts of zany constructions with your pipes and fittings. Store pieces in bucket.

Pop-Up Periscope

WHAT YOU NEED:
2 cardboard milk cartons (quart-size)
Scissors
2 purse-size rectangular mirrors
2 file cards
Double-stick tape
White glue

WHAT YOU DO:
1. Wash and dry milk cartons.
2. Fold open tops of cartons. Cut top off one carton.
3. Trim file cards to same width as mirrors.
4. Center a mirror on each card, leaving extra cardboard at both ends. Tape in place.
5. Cut a window in each carton as shown.
6. Position mirror cards in cartons as shown, folding edges to fit. Glue in place.
7. Put periscope together as shown, fitting carton without top inside carton with top. Periscope works two ways: in collapsed position to peer over short objects, or in pop-up position to see over tall objects.

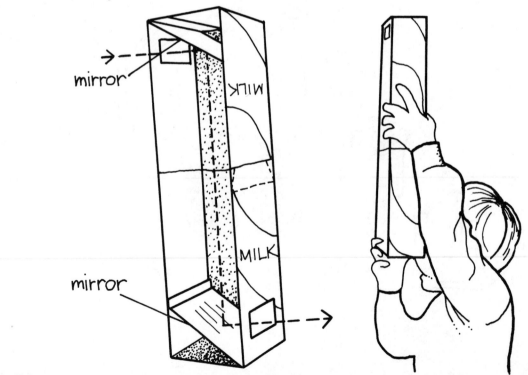

Pumping Station

WHAT YOU NEED:
Plastic ice cream bucket with lid
Scissors
Nail
Pumps from bottles of window cleaner, liquid soap, hand lotion,
  chocolate syrup, etc.

WHAT YOU DO:
1. Wash and dry the ice cream bucket and the pumps you have collected.
2. Cut a small circle out of ice cream bucket lid near rim. This is the water hole. Snap lid on bucket.
3. Poke nail hole in lid for each pump you have. Wiggle nail in each hole to make the hole larger.
4. Put a pump in each hole
5. Fill bucket with water through water hole. Set bucket in tub or sandbox. Squirt away!

Pushpin Loom

WHAT YOU NEED:
Rectangular meat tray (Styrofoam or cardboard)
Double-stick tape
Pushpins
Scissors
Heavy yarn
Blunt needle
Plastic fork

WHAT YOU DO:
1. Wash and dry meat tray. Turn it upside down.
2. Put double-stick tape along short ends of meat tray.
3. Press pushpins in along taped sides, spacing them about ½-inch apart.
4. Cut narrow notch under pin in lefthand corner on both ends for your yarn lock. Notch should look like upside-down *V*.
5. Cut off enough yarn to thread loom as shown, hooking ends of yarn in notches. These threads are your *warp*.
6. The needle is your *shuttle*. Thread yarn on shuttle and weave over and under warp threads. This cross-weave is called the *woof*. As you work, straighten weaving with plastic fork.
7. Pull out pushpins to take weaving off loom. Knot or fringe warp threads.
8. For variations, press pushpins in long sides of meat tray, or use a different shape or size tray.

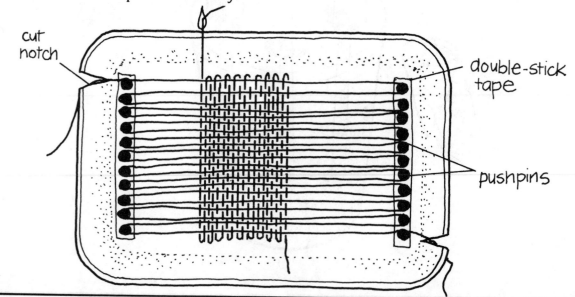

cut notch

double-stick tape

pushpins

Reflecting Shield

WHAT YOU NEED:
Box lid (largest you can find)
Grapefruit knife
Plastic wrap
Tape
Aluminum foil baking pans (pot pie pans, muffin pans, etc.)
Nail
Brass fasteners
Cardboard tube from wire pants hanger
Bike reflector

WHAT YOU DO:
1. Cut out window in top end of box lid with grapefruit knife.
2. Tape plastic wrap over back of window.
3. Arrange foil pans wherever you like on box lid. Poke two nail holes in each pan. Attach pans to box lid with brass fasteners.
4. Cut out two small holes opposite each other in side rims of box, just below window.
5. Insert cardboard tube in holes for a shield handle.
6. Poke two nail holes in top rim of shield. Insert bike reflector.
7. Hold shield in front of you as you walk a dangerous path. Who would dare attack?!

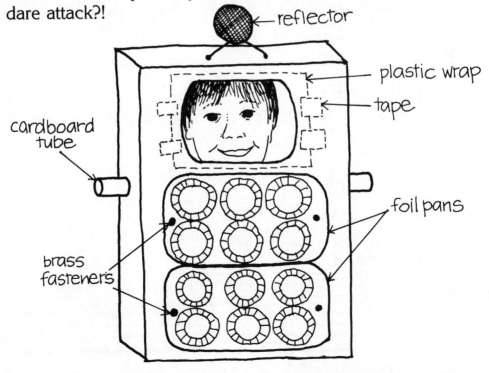

reflector

plastic wrap

tape

cardboard tube

foil pans

brass fasteners

River Raft

WHAT YOU NEED:
2 wooden pallets (available free at many stores)
Hammer
2 nails
Y-shaped branch
Plastic lid from ice cream bucket
Kitchen shears
Old broomstick
Strapping tape
Bamboo pole
Bandanna
2 spring-type clothespins

WHAT YOU DO:
1. Place pallets side-by-side on grass.
2. Nail Y-shaped branch to back of raft for oarlock.
3. Cut oar blade out of the inside of the plastic lid.
4. Tape oar blade onto broomstick with strapping tape. Fit oar into lock.
5. Clip bandanna onto bamboo pole with clothespins for flag. Brace flagpole between slats in raft with short branch.
6. Fill a water bottle, pack a snack, and head down river!

Roll-On Ramps

WHAT YOU NEED:
Yardstick
Pencil
3 or more cardboard soda trays
Kitchen shears
Toy cars or ball

WHAT YOU DO:
1. Use yardstick and pencil to draw lines on opposite rims of a soda tray, from bottom corner at one end to top corner at other end.
2. Cut away rims on these lines. Fold down rim at lower end to make a ramp. Make more ramps. You may also want to leave a soda tray uncut as a platform, or cut off all the rims to make a landing.
3. Turn trays upside down. Arrange end-to-end on floor, high rims touching.
4. Roll toy cars or a small ball along ramps. What action!

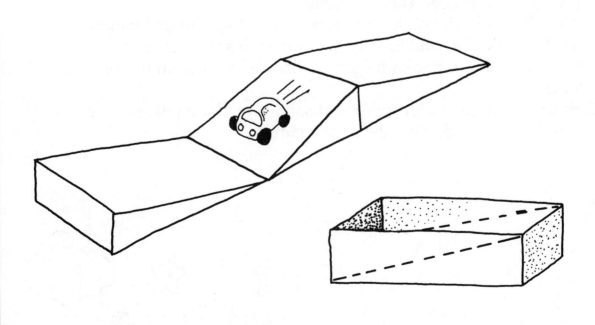

Sandbox Robot

WHAT YOU NEED:
2 plastic colanders with side handles
2 plastic milk carton tops
Nail
2 brass fasteners
2 coffee can lids
Ballpoint pen
Scissors
Paper punch
Wire handle from cardboard ice cream carton
Household sand toys (quart-size plastic carton, gelatin molds, big spoon, funnel, etc.)

WHAT YOU DO:
1. Wash and dry bottle tops. Poke nail hole in center of each top.
2. Turn one colander upside down. Attach bottle tops to colander with brass fasteners for the robot's eyes.
3. Trace sand fork pattern on each coffee can lid with ballpoint pen. Cut out sand forks.
4. Punch hole in top of each sand fork. Punch two holes opposite each other in plastic carton.
5. Fill second colander with sand toys.
6. Place first colander on top of second, rims together and handles lined up. Insert a sand fork up through each set of handles so tines point down. Hook wire bucket handle to holes on top of forks.
7. Head for the sand with your robot sand toys. For a pail, snap the robot's wire handle onto the plastic carton.

Sand Fork Pattern

Ship-to-Shore Pulley

WHAT YOU NEED:
Narrow rope
Small pulley with ring on bottom
Plastic ice cream bucket without lid
Twine
Scissors

WHAT YOU DO:
1. Slip pulley onto rope.
2. Tie rope with pulley between two supports (e.g., trees, clothesline poles, hooks, or fence posts).
3. Carefully snap off wire handle from ice cream bucket. Bend until rounded.
4. Slip bucket handle through pulley ring. Snap handle back on bucket.
5. Cut two equal lengths of twine at least as long as the pulley rope. Tie one piece onto each side of bucket handle.
6. Fill bucket with toys, supplies, snacks, or messages. Send bucket back and forth with your mates by taking turns pulling the twine. Don't let go of your own end, or you won't be able to retrieve the bucket!

Soda Tray Pinball

WHAT YOU NEED:
2 cardboard soda trays
Pushpins
Ballpoint pen
Small marbles

WHAT YOU DO:
1. Fit the bottom end of one soda tray inside the other soda tray. Let the top end lean on the rim of the other tray. (The upper tray should rest on a tilt.)
2. Stick pushpins wherever you like in the upper tray. Stick some in clusters of two or three.
3. Also stick two pushpins inside the bottom edge of the tray to divide into three sections.
4. Write score numbers in the sections along the bottom edge.
5. Players toss marbles at top of soda tray. Wherever marble lands, player gets number of points shown. Try to beat your own or someone else's highest score.

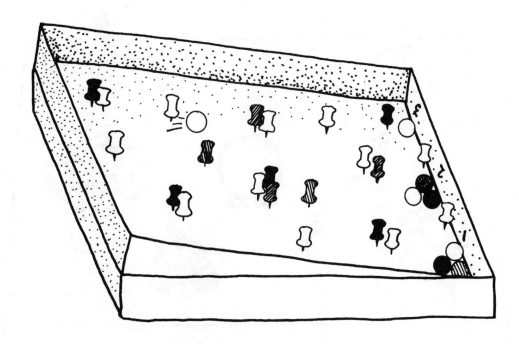

Sound Effects Board

WHAT YOU NEED:
Piece of scrap lumber (about 1' x 2')
Sandpaper or sanding sponge
Objects for sound effects (see suggestions in step 5)
Nail
Screw eyes (smallest size)
Shoelaces

WHAT YOU DO:
1. Sand smooth any rough edges on scrap lumber.
2. Collect objects that can be used to make familiar sounds. For example, clap two margarine tubs together for galloping horses. Crumple cellophane wrap for a crackling fire.
3. Arrange the items on the board. Poke a nail hole next to each object. Screw a screw eye into each hole.
4. Tie one end of a shoelace through each screw eye. Tie a sound object onto other end.
5. Pretend you're on the radio. Read a favorite story or tell a new one. Add sound effects whenever appropriate. After you finish a program, remove old objects and tie on new ones.

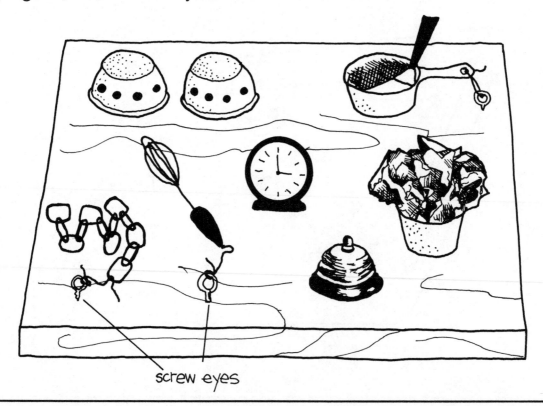

screw eyes

Space Station

WHAT YOU NEED:
2 cardboard cutting boards (used for sewing)
Nail
Brass fasteners (largest size)
Grapefruit knife
Blue and yellow construction paper
White glue
4 or more lids from peel-strip juice cans or canning jars
Hammer

WHAT YOU DO:
1. Overlap two end panels of cutting boards. Poke nail holes through both panels. Attach panels with brass fasteners.
2. Stand cutting boards in circle on floor for walls of space station.
3. Cut circular window out of one wall.
4. Cut moon and stars out of yellow paper. Glue onto blue paper. This is your screen. Glue screen onto another wall.
5. Hammer nail hole in center of each lid. Attach to wall of space station with brass fasteners. These are your control knobs.
6. Spot starry objects out the window of your space station as you orbit in space. Bring along some earthly comforts, like chairs, pillows, snacks, and games. To change the shape of your space station, simply move the folding panels.

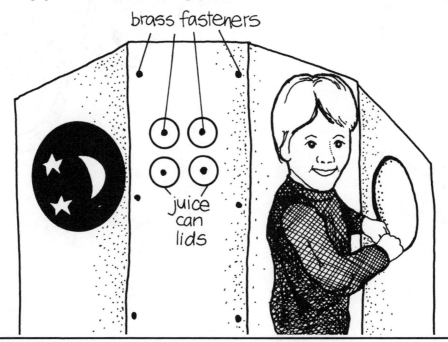

brass fasteners

juice can lids

Spinner Scope

WHAT YOU NEED:
Paper plates
Scissors
Watercolor markers
Pushpin
Unsharpened pencil with eraser top

WHAT YOU DO:
1. Cut out notches around edge of plates as shown.
2. Draw a design on each plate with markers. Draw a spiral, small circles close to each other, or a simple object, such as a fish.
3. Poke pushpin through center of plate, then into eraser end of pencil.
4. Stand in front of mirror. Spin pencil between hands as you peer through the notches. Each design will produce a different *optical illusion* as the spinning elements appear to merge.

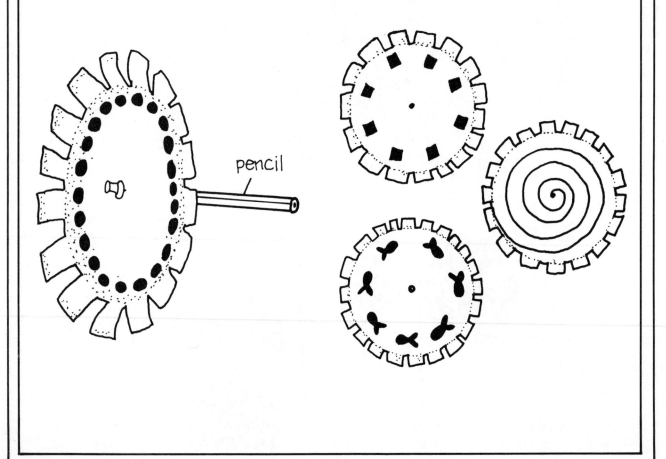

pencil

Splashing Star

WHAT YOU NEED:
Plastic lid
Ballpoint pen
Kitchen shears
Nail
String

WHAT YOU DO:
1. Draw star shape on plastic lid with ballpoint pen.
2. Cut out star.
3. Poke nail hole in center of star.
4. Cut off two 18″ pieces of string. Thread strings through hole in star. Knot ends together.
5. Fill sink or basin halfway with water.
6. Hold string and spin in circular motion to twist it.
7. Lower points of star in water and pull strings tightly. Splash! Experiment with other pointy shapes, such as triangles and parallelograms.

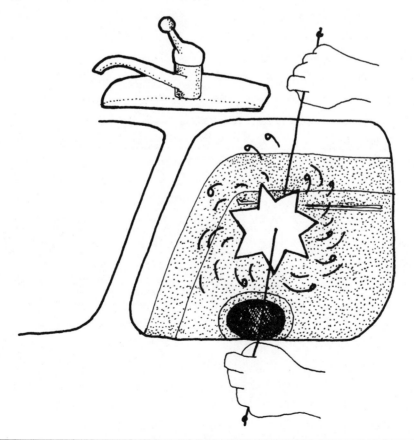

Straw Flute

WHAT YOU NEED:
Plastic straw
Scissors

WHAT YOU DO:
1. Pinch one end of the straw. Cut a tiny slit on both sides of the fold. This is your reed.
2. Fold over straw near bottom. Cut a very tiny hole in the corner of the fold.
3. Put reed in your mouth and blow with lips pressed together. Blow hard.
4. Hold finger over hole to change pitch. For more notes, cut additional tiny holes near end of straw. Hold finger over different holes while blowing.

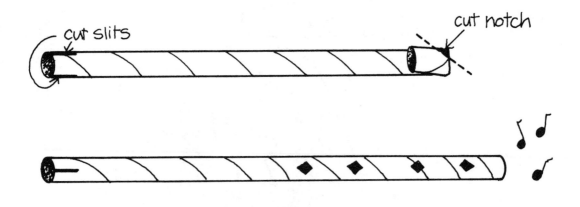

cut slits

cut notch

Terrific Tote

WHAT YOU NEED:
15 plastic soda can holders
Scissors
Yarn
3 yards twill tape (from sewing store)

WHAT YOU DO:
1. Lay out six plastic holders on table in two rows of three each.
2. Tie circles together at centers with yarn as shown. This is the front of your tote. Repeat for back.
3. Cut remaining three holders in half lengthwise. Connect each pair of half-holders end-to-end with yarn ties.
4. Make sides of tote by tying half-holders between front and back of tote. Do the same along the bottom of tote.
5. Cut twill tape in half. Weave one tape down one side, across bottom, and up other side on front of tote for added strength. Do same on back of tote.
6. Pull tape so straps are even. Knot together at top. Trim straps if they're too long. Then put something in your tote and tote it somewhere!

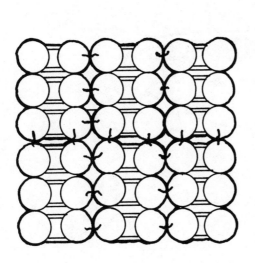 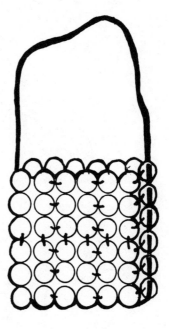

Thinking Cap

WHAT YOU NEED:
Plastic colander (without long handle)
Plastic funnel
Strapping tape
2 large pipe cleaners
2 practice golf balls (the kind with the holes)
Lid from peel-strip juice can or canning jar
Double-stick tape

WHAT YOU DO:
1. Turn colander upside down. Tape funnel on top.
2. Push a pipe cleaner through each golf ball. Fold down and twist ends to make strong antennas. Fasten antennas through front holes in colander as shown.
3. Stick lid to front of colander with double-stick tape. Put on your thinking cap. What are you thinking?

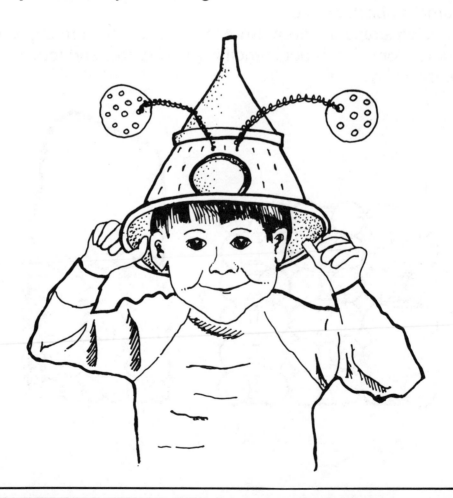

Trampoline Target

WHAT YOU NEED:
1-lb. coffee can without lid
Medium-sized balloon
Scissors
Large rubber band
4 cardboard egg flats (the kind that hold several dozen eggs)
Watercolor marker
Practice golf ball

WHAT YOU DO:
1. Cut neck off balloon. Stretch round part over top of coffee can. Secure with rubber band. This is your trampoline.
2. Make dots in a few egg sections in each flat with marker.
3. Arrange flats around trampoline.
4. Players take turns bouncing ball on the trampoline. If ball lands on a flat, player scores one point. If ball lands in a dotted section, player gets an extra point. Highest score after several rounds wins.

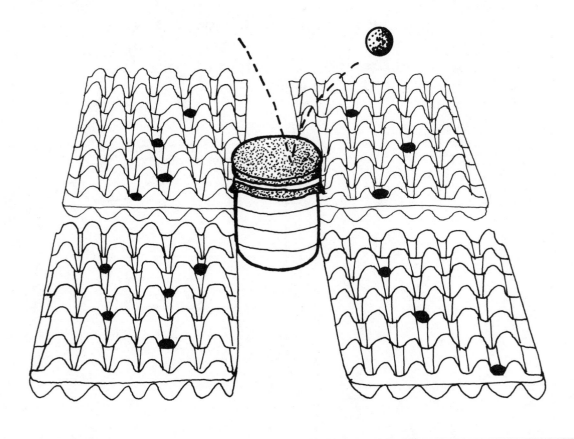

Weather Vane

WHAT YOU NEED:
Wood scrap or piece of corrugated cardboard
Styrofoam or wooden spool
White glue
Unsharpened pencil with eraser top
File card
Pencil
Scissors
Plastic straw
Thin nail
Straight pin

WHAT YOU DO:
1. Glue spool on center of wood scrap. Let dry.
2. Stand unsharpened pencil in spool, eraser end up.
3. Draw circle and triangle on file card and cut out.
4. Poke nail through middle of straw.
5. Insert pin down through nail holes and into eraser. Straw should sit loosely on pin.
6. Make parallel slits about ½" long in both ends of straw.
7. Fit circle cutout in one end of straw, triangle in the other.
8. Set weather vane outside and see which way it spins. Weight base with two rocks if it's really windy.

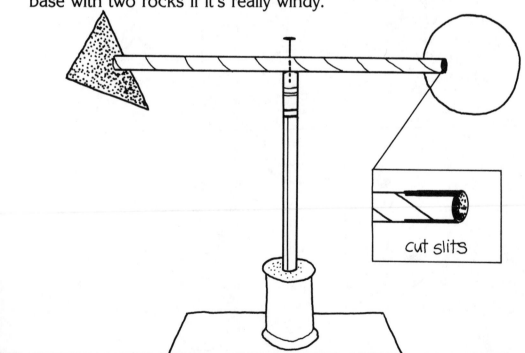

cut slits

Wind Meter

WHAT YOU NEED:
Paper plate
Hole punch (smallest hole size)
4 Styrofoam cups
4 inch-wide paper strips
4 brass fasteners
Styrofoam or wooden spool
White glue
Wood scrap or piece of corrugated cardboard
Unsharpened pencil with eraser top
Pushpin

WHAT YOU DO:
1. Punch four equidistant holes in rim of plate.
2. Glue paper strip around each cup, gluing ends together to form a tab as shown. Let dry.
3. Punch a hole in each tab.
4. Attach cups to plate through holes with brass fasteners.
5. Glue spool on center of wood scrap. Let dry.
6. Stand unsharpened pencil in spool, eraser end up.
7. Insert pushpin in center of plate. Wiggle to enlarge hole, then stick pushpin into eraser.
8. Set wind meter outside on a breezy day. How fast is the wind blowing? Measure in spins per minute. Weight base of wind meter with two rocks if it's really windy.

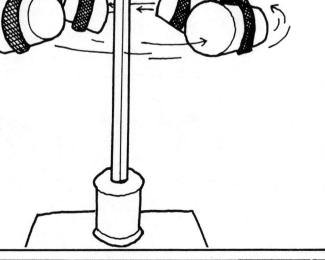

Wind Tunnel

WHAT YOU NEED:
Oatmeal carton without lid
Plastic wrap
Rubber band
Scissors
Air mattress pump
Lightweight materials (feathers, tissue paper, cottonballs, etc.)

WHAT YOU DO:
1. Tear off sheet of plastic wrap slightly wider than diameter of oatmeal carton.
2. Cut round hole in bottom of carton the same diameter as pump hose. Insert hose end.
3. Set carton on side. Place lightweight materials inside.
4. Cover open end with plastic wrap. Secure with rubber band.
5. Pump in air to see which objects fly.

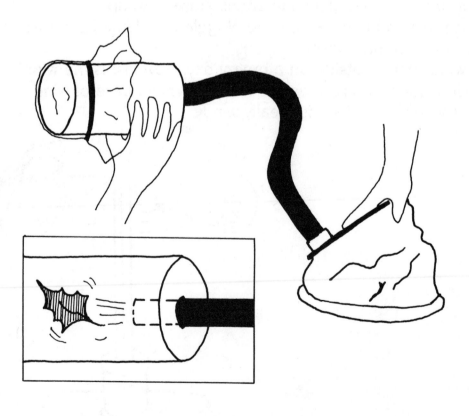